SPOILER ALERT

Bruce Willis Is Dead and 399 More Endings from Movies, TV, Books, and Life

Robb Pearlman

Lyons Press
Guilford, Connecticut
An imprint of Globe Pequot Press

Lyons Press is an imprint of Globe Pequot Press

Text design/layout: Maggie Peterson

Library of Congress Cataloging-in-Publication Data is available on file.

ISBN 978-0-7627-7384-8

Printed in the United States of America

10 9 8 7 6 5 4 3 2 1

1.

The hot chick is a dude.

THE CRYING GAME

2.

You will forget to clear your browsing history before sharing your computer with your mom.

3.

The rednecks kill the woman pretending to be a man.

BOYS DON'T CRY

4.

Florida kills the woman who killed all the men.

MONSTER

5.

The woman pretending to be a man pretending to be a woman kills!

VICTOR/VICTORIA

6.

Clarice kills the man who wants to be a woman and who killed all the women.

SILENCE OF THE LAMBS

7.

She kills her husband with a leg of lamb and then feeds the murder weapon to the authorities.

LAMB TO THE SLAUGHTER

8.

They feed everyone to everyone and then they die.

SWEENEY TODD

9.

You will pay more for your friend's birthday dinner than you anticipated.

10.

To Serve Man is a cookbook.

THE TWILIGHT ZONE

11.

He will forget to tell you he's bringing his boss home for dinner.

12.

He will tell you he has a client dinner.

13.

She will know you're lying about your client dinner.

14.

It's made of people.

SOYLENT GREEN

15.

You will like him more when he's angry.

THE HULK

16.

You will grow and understand
that you will need new pants.

MASTERING THE ART OF FRENCH COOKING

17.

**You will grow to understand
that the oven is not a place
to store your pants.**

THE JOY OF COOKING

18.

Audrey Hepburn and the guy from
The A-Team kiss in the back of a cab
while a wet pussy tries to escape.

BREAKFAST AT TIFFANY'S

19.

You will never make him a better kisser.

20.

Tiffany's does not serve food.

21.

Shirley MacLaine, unable to handle her
love for Audrey Hepburn, hangs herself.

THE CHILDREN'S HOUR

22.

They drive off a cliff.

THELMA AND LOUISE

23.

Your car will lose value
the moment you get it home.

24.

Mark Ruffalo oversteps; Julianne Moore and Annette Bening reconcile enough to drop Alice off at college before she heads to Wonderland.

THE KIDS ARE ALL RIGHT

25.

Blair buys Eastland.

THE FACTS OF LIFE

26.

Kelly and the boys go off to college together, Lisa goes into anonymity, and Jessie goes on to a successful career as a bi-curious Las Vegas showgirl who enjoys uncomfortable sex in pools with Kyle MacLachlan.

SAVED BY THE BELL

27.

Strippers are nice to everyone.

28.

You will lose money in Las Vegas.

29.

Glenn Close wins her wager,
but everyone discovers what a *chienne*
she is, and society shuns her.

DANGEROUS LIAISONS

30.

_____.

MATCH GAME

31.

Playing video games will leave your hands arthritic and gnarled.

32.

Picard solves Q's timeline puzzles and joins his crew for a poker game, but is unable to stop the millions of dollars wasted on future big-screen adaptations.

STAR TREK: THE NEXT GENERATION

33.

Your parents let you win.

34.

The crew makes it back home; you finally emerge from your mom's basement.

STAR TREK: VOYAGER

35.

Your parents want you out of the house.

36.

Sam never makes it home.

QUANTUM LEAP

37.

Miss Daisy winds up in a nursing home, where she's visited by her BFF, Hoke.

DRIVING MISS DAISY

38.

That piercing is going to look really stupid when you're 80.

39.

Guy Pearce killed his wife.

MEMENTO

40.

You are going to regret that tattoo.

41.

Mildred Pierce realizes her daughter is such
an ungrateful brat she admits it was Veda
who killed Monte.

MILDRED PIERCE

42.

La femme n'est pas morte.

TELL NO ONE

43.

May dies, Newland and his son arrive
in Paris to visit Ellen, but Newland can't
go in.

THE AGE OF INNOCENCE

44.

Fantine, Javert, Eponine, and Valjean all die.
Cosette and Marius get married.

LES MISERABLES

45.

Something is going to go wrong on your wedding day.

46.

Bella marries Edward.

THE TWILIGHT SAGA

47.

Harriet marries Robert and Emma marries George.

EMMA

48.

Shirley marries a mystery man, leaving
Laverne alone in what becomes
an inappropriately named vehicle for
Penny Marshall's slapstick prowess.

LAVERNE AND SHIRLEY

49.

Debra Winger dies,
Shirley MacLaine loses it,
everyone laughs.

TERMS OF ENDEARMENT

50.

**Julia Roberts dies,
Sally Field loses it,
everyone laughs.**

STEEL MAGNOLIAS

51.

You will laugh at the wrong time.

52.

Jack dies and becomes part of the hotel.

THE SHINING

53.

Sounder crawls under the porch to die.

SOUNDER

54.

Beth dies.

LITTLE WOMEN

55.

You are going to die.

56.

Angel dies, Mimi lives, and nobody sells out.

RENT

57.

They will be out of stock.

58.

It was costume jewelry.

"THE NECKLACE"

59.

He sells his watch to buy her a comb, and she sells her hair to buy him a watch fob.

"THE GIFT OF THE MAGI"

60.

Nobody's watching.

WATCHMEN

61.

Nobody watched.

WATCHMEN

62.

You will not want to look at what's going on in the attic.

FLOWERS IN THE ATTIC

63.

They look in the attic.

THE DIARY OF ANNE FRANK

64.

Rochester's wife has been locked in the attic and burns down the house.

JANE EYRE

65.

The call is coming from inside the house.

WHEN A STRANGER CALLS

66.

The crystal phone booth protects Superman from the power-zapping rays.

SUPERMAN 2

67.

Your cell phone is shooting tumor-causing rays
into your head.

68.

Barbara Stanwyck shoots the dad from *My Three Sons*, but he kills her before dying.

DOUBLE INDEMNITY

69.

O. J. Simpson dies, and Barbra Streisand's first and second husbands escape captivity and run to their memorial service, exposing the government's cover-up.

CAPRICORN ONE

70.

Barbra and Robert Redford, long-divorced, meet in front of the Plaza, exchange pleasantries, and part.

THE WAY WE WERE

71.

**You
are the reason
your parents divorced.**

72.

Your parents
will never truly understand
you.

73.

Norman Bates dresses up like his mother and kills people.

PSYCHO

74.

Nobody understands modern art,
they just pretend to.

75.

Dorian Gray tears into the painting, killing himself.

THE PICTURE OF DORIAN GRAY

76.

Dorian Gray betrays them all.

THE LEAGUE OF EXTRAORDINARY GENTLEMEN

77.

It was all just a misunderstanding!

THREE'S COMPANY

78.

They all dance.

FOOTLOOSE

79.

Some of them dance.

A CHORUS LINE

80.

She never stops dancing.

THE RED SHOES

81.

He becomes a professional dancer.

BILLY ELLIOT

82.

They never dance again.

WEST SIDE STORY

83.

The swan dies.

SWAN LAKE

84.

Natalie Portman dies.

BLACK SWAN

85.

Your brother will be dying to come out halfway through.

BURLESQUE

86.

Jack is the baby Miss Prism left in the train station, making him Lady Bracknell's nephew and Algernon's brother.

THE IMPORTANCE OF BEING EARNEST

87.

Forgetting you at the rest stop wasn't a complete accident.

)

88.

She came tumbling after.

"JACK AND JILL"

89.

Jack Nicholson admits to ordering the code red, and, despite his warning, we can handle the truth.

A FEW GOOD MEN

90.

Briony doesn't tell the truth
until after Cecilia and Robbie are dead.

ATONEMENT

91.

You will forget the names
of most of your sorority sisters.

92.

You will try to remember.

THE FANTASTICKS

Robb Pearlman

93.

You will miss the toilet.

94.

Guinevere has an affair with Lancelot, driving Arthur to distraction, Camelot into the toilet, and herself to a nunnery.

CAMELOT

95.

The guy who played Nite Owl in *Watchmen* and Kate Winslet end their affair just as the guy who played Rorschach in *Watchmen* castrates himself.

LITTLE CHILDREN

96.

Kate lets go of Leo's hand and goes on to lead a full and happy life.

TITANIC

97.

Leo thinks Kate has let go of her needs and desires right before she dies from giving herself an at-home abortion.

REVOLUTIONARY ROAD

98.

Leo lets go of his runaway train
of a wife, (maybe) finishes the job and
(maybe) goes home to his kids. Maybe.
You'll go mental.

INCEPTION

99.

Leo's a mental patient on the island.

SHUTTER ISLAND

100.

They are rescued from the island. Except for Piggy. And that kid who looks like Leo.

THE LORD OF THE FLIES

101.

Everyone dies on the island—but some of them
sort of don't, while others come back.
It's confusing.

LOST

102.

Jesus dies. Then he comes back.
Then he disappears.
Then the choir sings.

THE NEW TESTAMENT

103.

Effie tells them she's not going, but she does, and they keep singing.
Then she comes back, and they sing some more.

DREAMGIRLS

104.

Ralphie gets his gun. The family gets serenaded at a Chinese restaurant by ethnically stereotyped waiters.
TBS has Christmas Day programming for the next twenty years.

A CHRISTMAS STORY

105.

There is no Santa Claus.

106.

A child, a lunatic, and an activist judge convert the citizens of New York City into Santa-believers.

MIRACLE ON 34TH STREET

107.

You will hold off breaking up with your boyfriend until after the holidays so you don't have to be alone.

108.

You will hold off breaking up with your girlfriend until after the holidays so you can still get gifts from her.

109.

Hanukkah is not as good as Christmas.

110.

Teabing is one of the bad guys.

THE DA VINCI CODE

111.

Ewan MacGregor is one of the bad guys.

ANGELS AND DEMONS

Robb Pearlman

112.

**The movie is not as good
as the book.**

113.

The book is not as good
as the movie.

114.

Hookers only have hearts of gold in the movies.

115.

He turns everything to gold.

KING MIDAS

116.

Dorothy marries Blanche's uncle Lucas. Blanche, Rose, and Sophia get spun-off into their own ill-conceived and short-lived series.

THE GOLDEN GIRLS

117.

B. J. can't say goodbye, but Hawkeye sees it spelled out in rocks on his way up in a helicopter. Father Mulcahy, Colonel Potter, and Klinger get spun off into their own ill-conceived and short-lived series.

M*A*S*H

118.

He never gets the boulder up the mountain.

"SISYPHUS"

119.

**Humphrey Bogart practically pushes
Ingrid Bergman onto the plane
and begins a beautiful friendship
with Claude Rains.**

CASABLANCA

120.

Monica and Chandler move to the suburbs;
Rachel and Ross are each others' lobsters;
Phoebe marries Paul Rudd; Joey gets
spun off into his own ill-conceived
and short-lived series.

FRIENDS

121.

Eve, who finally has everything she wants, is about to get Eve'd by Phoebe.

ALL ABOUT EVE

122.

Your Facebook friends aren't really your friends.

123.

Nobody reads your blog.

124.

Mark Zuckerberg makes billions from our inability to keep anything private.

THE SOCIAL NETWORK

125.

The hot girl turns out to be a middle-aged
mom; millions of Internet daters nod
in silent recognition.

CATFISH

126.

The old woman is the devil.

DEVIL

127.

Mrs. Voorhees is the killer.

FRIDAY THE 13TH

128.

Milla Jovovich is the fifth element.

THE FIFTH ELEMENT

129.

Your mom was the Tooth Fairy.

130.

You will actively seek out sales on mom jeans.

131.

Your children will disappoint you.

132.

Laura Palmer was killed by her father.

TWIN PEAKS

133.

Your father played Hide and Seek to give himself a break from you.

134.

Your children will resent you.

135.

Tilda Swinton leaves her family for her dead son's best friend.

I AM LOVE

136.

She leaves her life behind.

A DOLL'S HOUSE

137.

She leaves her life.

HEDDA GABLER

138.

You will leave a balance on your gift cards.

139.

You should not leave the house wearing that.

140.

You will be underdressed.

141.

Those jeans do make you look fat.

142.

Black will never be as slimming as you want it to be.

143.

You will say something racist.

144.

**You will eat the entire bucket of popcorn
by yourself.**

145.

You will never check everything off your bucket list.

146.

The King and Anna can never be together, so he drops dead.

THE KING AND I

147.

Simba returns and defeats Scar.

THE LION KING

148.

The king returns.

THE LORD OF THE RINGS: THE RETURN OF THE KING

149.

**You will not wear your class ring
six months after graduation.**

150.

The proverbial postman proverbially rang twice: once for Cora, now dead, and again for Frank, on his way to execution.

THE POSTMAN ALWAYS RINGS TWICE

151.

Mickey Rourke goes back into the ring despite doctor's orders.

THE WRESTLER

152.

Professional wrestling isn't real.

153.

Told you so.

THE POSTMAN ALWAYS RINGS TWICE, 1981

154.

**Sitting too close to the television
has irreparably harmed your eyesight.**

155.

The new owners of WJM fire everyone but Ted.

THE MARY TYLER MOORE SHOW

156.

Howard Beale dies on live television and ratings soar.

NETWORK

157.

Reality television isn't real.

158.

She'd rather watch television.

159.

The ghost/monster/beast is a greedy guy in a costume.

SCOOBY-DOO

160.

They get away with it.

OCEAN'S 11

161.

They don't get away with it.

ROPE

162.

Richard Gere and Diane Lane drive to the police station. They don't go in, they just drive there.

UNFAITHFUL

163.

If Woody had gone right to the police, this would never have happened.

BUNCO BUSTERS

164.

Sergeant Trotter isn't a policeman at all.
He's the murderer.

THE MOUSETRAP

165.

Achilles kills Hector, who is buried in Troy.

THE ILIAD

166.

You would kill to be buried
in a Hector-Achilles sandwich.

TROY

167.

Angelina Jolie really is a Russian agent.

SALT

168.

Everyone noticed your pit stains.

169.

A flop-sweating Dustin Hoffman keeps the kid,
and Meryl Streep disappears.

KRAMER VS. KRAMER

170.

**Ellen Page gives up the kid,
and Jason Bateman disappears.**

JUNO

171.

Sophie chose to save her son, then she and Nathan choose to kill themselves.

SOPHIE'S CHOICE

172.

The mother and the kids are the ghosts, not the others.

THE OTHERS

173.

She will turn into her mother.

174.

Your mother will call you
when you're having sex.

175.

You will be caught in the middle of a fight
between your wife and your mother.

176.

You will choose the wrong side.

177.

You will have to choose someone to pull the plug for you.

178.

You will not be able to pull an all-nighter after the age of 35.

179.

You will suffer from insomnia after the age of 35.

180.

An almost-too-old for action films Han Solo
throws the device into the river after his
wife is freed and the girl is shot.

FRANTIC

181.

His mother is shot by hunters, so he goes to live with his somewhat distant father.

BAMBI

182.

Wendy, John, and Michael return to London and grow up.

PETER PAN

Robb Pearlman

183.

Ofelia remains a child forever.

PAN'S LABYRINTH

184.

Children will prefer the box
in which the gift came.

185.

You will have to ask your children for help
to figure out technology.

186.

You will not realize that you forgot to put
your "out of office" message on your work
email until the last day of your vacation.

187.

You will accidentally sign up
for email newsletters.

188.

You will accidentally reply all.

Robb Pearlman

189.

The IT guy thinks you're an idiot.

190.

The aliens are defeated by a computer virus.

INDEPENDENCE DAY

191.

The aliens are defeated by a rhinovirus.

WAR OF THE WORLDS

192.

Rosebud is a sled.

CITIZEN KANE

193.

Thanks to the old black-and-white
Hollywood rule of "evil must be punished,"
Rhoda inexplicably goes to the pier
in the middle of a thunderstorm
and gets hit by lightning.

THE BAD SEED

194.

But Rhoda totally gets away with it on Broadway.

THE BAD SEED

195.

Rhoda Morgenstern's mother, dressed as Truman Capote, did it.

MURDER BY DEATH

196.

Miss Scarlet killed Mr. Boddy; or Mrs. Peacock killed Mr. Boddy; or Mr. Green killed Mr. Boddy. Depends on which ending you see.

CLUE

197.

Everyone did it.

MURDER ON THE ORIENT EXPRESS

Robb Pearlman

198.

Everybody does it.

199.

The orangutan did it.

"MURDERS IN THE RUE MORGUE"

200.

You're the only person who does it.

201.

Bonnie Bedelia did it and threw off the cops by implanting into the corpse the, um, DNA she'd been saving from her and Indiana Jones's marital relations.

PRESUMED INNOCENT

202.

Archie regrets driving Edith to the point of death and sort-of tells her that he loves her, but then she dies while the show's retooled, and he goes on to star in *Archie Bunker's Place*.

ALL IN THE FAMILY

203.

They become more human in appearance and behavior.

ANIMAL FARM

204.

Charlotte dies, and her hundreds of newly orphaned children, Wilbur, and you learn the cold reality of death.

CHARLOTTE'S WEB

205.

The children and Johnny Depp find Neverland, inasmuch as becoming an orphan can be called Neverland.

FINDING NEVERLAND

206.

Johnny Depp is who he's been pretending to be.

THE TOURIST

207.

You will fake it.

208.

You will never know whether she fakes it.

209.

Glinda finally divulges crucial information,
the wizard's a fake, and Dorothy decides
there's no place like home.

THE WIZARD OF OZ

210.

Glinda and Elphaba had rich and
interesting lives of their own before
Dorothy and her friends showed up,
thankyouverymuch.

WICKED

211.

Your mother knew you were a friend
of Dorothy since you were five.

212.

One straight guy looks better; millions of
women hit gay bars in search of new
best friends.

QUEER EYE FOR THE STRAIGHT GUY

213.

You turned your first boyfriend gay.

214.

You will be the main character
in a cautionary tale.

215.

Carton is beheaded.

A TALE OF TWO CITIES

216.

Gwyneth Paltrow's head is in the box.

SE7EN

217.

Shakespeare falls in love.

SHAKESPEARE IN LOVE

218.

You will feel miserable about your life after
watching a romantic comedy alone.

219.

Lady Macbeth was the brains of the operation.

MACBETH

Robb Pearlman

220.

Sissy Spacek was the brains of the operation.

IN THE BEDROOM

221.

Finger-operated folded-paper fortune-
telling devices cannot accurately predict
whom you'll marry.

222.

You were the first man she met
after she lowered her standards.

223.

Elizabeth and Darcy marry.

PRIDE AND PREJUDICE

224.

Elinor and Edward marry, which is sweet.
Marianne and Colonel Brandon marry,
which is worrisome, given the huge
age difference coupled with the
average lifespan back then.

SENSE AND SENSIBILITY

225.

Avdotya and Razumikhin marry, and
Sonya follows Raskolnikov to Siberia;
you rationalize that they have a better
chance for something long-term than
Marianne and Colonel Brandon do.

CRIME AND PUNISHMENT

226.

Westley and Buttercup share tru wuv and live happily ever after.

THE PRINCESS BRIDE

227.

Romeo and Juliet share a bond of true love but don't live, and nobody's happy after.

ROMEO AND JULIET

228.

Harry Potter defeats Voldemort and marries Ginny Weasley.

THE HARRY POTTER SERIES

229.

Harry sees an analyst and blinds all the horses.

EQUUS

230.

Harry gets back in the saddle, buys a self-help book, and succeeds.

HOW TO SUCCEED IN BUSINESS WITHOUT REALLY TRYING

231.

You will not be able to get change without a purchase.

232.

Alex moves to New York and changes his name before going to work at City Hall.

FAMILY TIES

233.

Alex (now Mike) leaves Charlie Sheen in charge of City Hall.

SPIN CITY

234.

Michael Douglas and Charlie Sheen go to jail.

WALL STREET

235.

Gerard Butler had been using a tunnel to get out of jail.

LAW ABIDING CITIZEN

236.

You will get lost.

237.

They remain lost. In space.

LOST IN SPACE

238.

Ripley and the cat survive.

ALIEN

239.

Though no one can hear you scream in space, you can hear the final nail being hammered into the coffin.

STAR TREK: ENTERPRISE

240.

It's *Pocahontas*. In space. And blue.

AVATAR

241.

Gargamel never captures the Smurfs.

THE SMURFS

242.

**You will not understand why you
liked the books you liked as a child.**

243.

See readers fail standardized testing.

DICK AND JANE

244.

Atticus loses the case. Not-a-nutjob Boo saves Scout and Jem from revenge-seeking actual nutjob Bob Ewell.

TO KILL A MOCKINGBIRD

245.

Jack Nicholson gets lobotomized, and the Chief escapes by throwing a sink out the window.

ONE FLEW OVER THE CUCKOO'S NEST

246.

Stanley rapes Blanche, Blanche goes into a mental institution, and Stella stops responding to Stanley's bellowing.

A STREETCAR NAMED DESIRE

247.

Halle Berry's not the crazy one.

GOTHIKA

248.

Your therapist thinks you're nuts.

249.

The hippies' wacky plan to switch places goes haywire when the wrong one gets sent to Vietnam; they sing as a generation loses its credibility.

HAIR

250.

You will lose hair where you want it.

251.

You will grow hair where you don't want it.

252.

Tortoise beats hare.

253.

Rabbit beats duck.

RABBIT SEASON

254.

George tells Lennie about the rabbits.
And then kills him.

OF MICE AND MEN

255.

Your dad, not the Easter Bunny, hid the eggs.

256.

Nobody could put him together again.

"HUMPTY DUMPTY"

Robb Pearlman

257.

Everything on your body is going to sag.
Everything.

258.

The prince returns to his planet, sans body, and the narrator is rescued from the desert.

THE LITTLE PRINCE

259.

The narrator and Tyler Durden are the same person.

FIGHT CLUB

260.

Verbal Kint and Keyser Söze are the same person.

THE USUAL SUSPECTS

261.

The Kobayashi Maru is unwinnable.

STAR TREK II: THE WRATH OF KHAN

262.

Unless you cheat.

STAR TREK, 2009

263.

Daniel Day-Lewis drinks everyone's milkshake and beats Paul Dano to death with a bowling pin.

THERE WILL BE BLOOD

264.

That's not quite
what the Founding Fathers meant.

THE CONSTITUTION OF THE UNITED STATES OF AMERICA

Robb Pearlman

265.

The candidate whose name you stick on your bumper will lose.

266.

Darth Vader is Luke's father.

THE EMPIRE STRIKES BACK

267.

Luke and Leia are twins.

RETURN OF THE JEDI

268.

The kiss between Luke and Leia is, in retrospect, a little unsettling.

STAR WARS

269.

He really really loves his mother and kills his father.

"OEDIPUS"

270.

She kills her mother.

CARRIE

271.

She kills her daughter.

BELOVED

272.

The sons sell the land out from under their father.

THE GOOD EARTH

273.

Boardwalk and Park Place
are not the best properties.

274.

The previews showed the best parts of the movie.

275.

The entire film took place in Tim Robbins's mind as he was dying in Vietnam.

JACOB'S LADDER

276.

It contains microfilm.

THE MALTESE FALCON

277.

Nobody wants to see
your vacation photos.

278.

**Visiting EPCOT is nothing like
visiting another country.**

279.

The trifurcated Fellowship ventures deeper into Middle Earth as a second world war begins.

THE LORD OF THE RINGS: THE TWO TOWERS

280.

The king stops stammering long enough to make a speech that brings England into World War II.

THE KING'S SPEECH

281.

Rolfe rats the von Trapps out to the Nazis.

THE SOUND OF MUSIC

282.

Private Ryan is saved.

SAVING PRIVATE RYAN

283.

Robert DeNiro saves Jodie Foster and, after recuperating from his injuries and being hailed a hero, goes back to driving a taxi.

TAXI DRIVER

284.

Jodie Foster's kid was stashed with the snack mix and little bottles of wine.

FLIGHTPLAN

285.

Karen Black lands the plane.

AIRPORT

286.

Robert Hays lands the plane.

AIRPLANE!

287.

The plane lands in the ocean.

AIRPORT '77

288.

Hilary Swank never really lands the plane, per se, anywhere.

AMELIA

289.

Jack Lemmon moves on to a plane where neither days nor dates hold meaning.

TUESDAYS WITH MORRIE

290.

You will wish you checked the expiration date.

291.

You will look too old to be carded by the bouncer.

292.

You will want to start eating dinner at 4:30.

293.

It takes place on Earth in the future.

THE PLANET OF THE APES

Robb Pearlman

294.

**It takes place in the past,
and it's going to happen again.**

BATTLESTAR GALACTICA

295.

It doesn't happen again.

CAPRICA

296.

You will have to tell him
it happens to every man.

297.

It doesn't happen to every man.

298.

The man reaches the end of the road.

THE ROAD

299.

Eva and Tom die. Cassy and Emmeline reach freedom in Canada.

UNCLE TOM'S CABIN

300.

Huck and Tom knew Jim was a free man but didn't tell him about it. Huck heads west to seek more adventures, but you know it's because Jim's totally going to kick his ass.

THE ADVENTURES OF HUCKLEBERRY FINN

301.

Speaking with a blaccent accentuates
how hopelessly white you are.

302.

Wile E. Coyote never catches the Road Runner.

EVERYUM SATURDAYMORNINGICUS

303.

All those years of studying calculus
were a complete waste of time.

304.

You will regret wearing that outfit
for your yearbook photo.

305.

The "private" photos you gave
your boyfriend will make their way
onto the Internet.

306.

He was naked.

THE EMPEROR'S NEW CLOTHES

307.

**Your dry cleaner makes fun of
your clothes.**

308.

Jeff Bridges goes to A.A., cleans up his life,
but doesn't get Maggie Gyllenhaal back.

CRAZY HEART

309.

Maggie shot Mr. Burns.

THE SIMPSONS

310.

Pam dreamt an entire season.

DALLAS

311.

Bob dreamt an entire series.

NEWHART

312.

Kevin Costner builds it, and they come.

FIELD OF DREAMS

313.

Roark is found not guilty, and Wynand
commissions him to build a
very phallic building.

THE FOUNTAINHEAD

314.

Jamal becomes a millionaire.

SLUMDOG MILLIONAIRE

315.

Money can buy happiness.

316.

They live in a gated community in modern times.

THE VILLAGE

317.

The villagers, not the creature,
are the true monsters.

FRANKENSTEIN

318.

Your town mixes recycling and regular garbage.

319.

They get out of the woods.

INTO THE WOODS

320.

They get out of Africa.

OUT OF AFRICA

321.

Whoopi leaves Danny Glover and his abuse to open a shop that makes the first pair of traveling pants (that fit everyone). Her sister and children return from Africa.

THE COLOR PURPLE

322.

She OWNs us all.

THE OPRAH WINFREY SHOW

323.

There isn't a dry smize in the house.

THE TYRA BANKS SHOW

324.

According to the ratings, everyone thought it had already been canceled.

ACCORDING TO JIM

325.

It ends.

THE NEVERENDING STORY

326.

It's a very special ending.

BLOSSOM

327.

It. Never. Ends.

A.I.: ARTIFICIAL INTELLIGENCE

328.

It just . . . sort of en–

THE SOPRANOS

329.

Don't bother sending in the clowns. They're already here.

A LITTLE NIGHT MUSIC

330.

The guy from *Hung* kills his kid, sort-of girlfriend, and two senior citizens seconds before the military comes through, clearing away the mist and the monsters.

THE MIST

331.

Al Gore was right.

332.

He loses.

ROCKY

333.

He wins.

ROCKY 2

334.

Marky Mark wins. Neither Batman nor the Funky Bunch take any credit for it.

THE FIGHTER

335.

He wins and celebrates
by bedding a woman named
[insert sexual innuendo here].

ANY JAMES BOND MOVIE

336.

James Franco cuts off his arm; you throw up.

127 HOURS

337.

James Franco co-hosts; you want to throw up.

THE 83RD ANNUAL ACADEMY AWARDS

338.

Anne Hathaway tells Heath Ledger, who looks and sounds more homeless than ever, that Jake Gyllenhaal's dead.

BROKEBACK MOUNTAIN

339.

Based on the amount of time you spend at Starbucks, people think you're homeless, not a hard-working novelist.

340.

You should have gone when you had the chance.

341.

You will never get that opportunity again.

342.

Death passes over the Hebrews and lands on Lil' Yul.

THE TEN COMMANDMENTS

343.

Moses never gets to the Promised Land.

THE OLD TESTAMENT

344.

You will wish you brought a magazine.

345.

He never arrives.

WAITING FOR GODOT

346.

People will arrive early to your party.

347.

Not everyone will RSVP to your party.

348.

Winston accepts his fate and the party.

1984

349.

You will not want to go into work the day
after getting drunk at the holiday party.

350.

After a long day and night of fighting, drunk Ralph Richardson, very drunk Jason Robards, and consumptive Dean Stockwell put the fun in family dysfunction by sitting and listening to high-as-a-kite Katharine Hepburn ramble about how beautiful she was.

LONG DAY'S JOURNEY INTO NIGHT

351.

**You should have listened
to your mother.**

352.

Elizabeth Taylor finally gets through the story about cousin Sebastian being eaten alive by tropical rentboys when, suddenly, Katharine Hepburn goes crazy.

SUDDENLY, LAST SUMMER

353.

Cousin Oliver kills a good show.

THE BRADY BUNCH

354.

Emma kills herself by drinking arsenic.

MADAME BOVARY

355.

Anna kills herself by throwing herself in front of a train.

ANNA KARENINA

356.

Septimus kills himself by jumping out of a window, but that doesn't stop Clarissa from throwing a fabulous party.

MRS. DALLOWAY

357.

Jennifer commits suicide, Neely becomes a hopeless drug addict, Anne returns home, and drag queens across the country wrap their sequined shawls around a reference point.

VALLEY OF THE DOLLS

358.

Melanie dies, Ashley collapses, Scarlett decides to think about it all tomorrow, Rhett doesn't give a damn, and Southerners wrap their Confederate flags around a reference point.

GONE WITH THE WIND

359.

Jody has to kill Flag to put him out of his misery.

THE YEARLING

360.

The Federation joins the Romulans and Klingons to overthrow the Dominion, and this sentence provides you with the perfect ice breaker at Comic-Con.

STAR TREK: DEEP SPACE NINE

361.

The bomb goes off and The Penguin breaks his glasses before he can read anything.

THE TWILIGHT ZONE

362.

The band breaks up.

THAT THING YOU DO!

363.

She doesn't like that thing you do
with your tongue.

364.

**He doesn't like that thing you do
with your teeth.**

365.

Your dentist knows you don't floss.

366.

Charlie and his grandfather escape a psychedelic candy sweatshop.

CHARLIE AND THE CHOCOLATE FACTORY

367.

You will never be able to bake a pie
as well as your grandmother did.

368.

**The Beanie Babies your grandmother
left you in her will are worthless.**

369.

The toys you donated to charity are worth
thousands of dollars.

370.

Woody and the gang accept Buzz into their family.

TOY STORY

371.

Woody, Buzz, and the gang accept Jessie and Bullseye into their family.

TOY STORY 2

372.

You weep uncontrollably as you realize that Woody, Buzz, and the gang are part of your family and family is the only thing that really matters.

TOY STORY 3

373.

Doesn't really matter.

FAMILY MATTERS

374.

Big Daddy learns that he's dying, Big Mamma grows a pair, and Liz and Paul deny his rampant alcoholism and latent homosexuality long enough to head into the bedroom.

CAT ON A HOT TIN ROOF

375.

Justin Bartha's been on the roof of the hotel the entire time.

THE HANGOVER

376.

Things can get worse.

377.

You cannot make him a better man.

378.

You remind her of her father.

379.

Magwitch is Pip's benefactor and Estella's father.

GREAT EXPECTATIONS

380.

Michael takes over his father's business.

THE GODFATHER

381.

Fredo isn't as safe in the boat as he thinks he is and goes to the Great Beyond.

THE GODFATHER PART 2

382.

Frodo finds safety in a boat
and goes deeper into Middle Earth.

THE LORD OF THE RINGS: THE FELLOWSHIP OF THE RING

383.

**Your pet goldfish see you;
they just don't care.**

384.

He finds Nemo.

FINDING NEMO

385.

**If you're not in a pool,
you're swimming in fish pee.**

386.

Santiago goes 84 days before catching a giant fish, and you go more than a hundred pages before realizing the only thing more boring than fishing is reading about it.

THE OLD MAN AND THE SEA

387.

Gene Hackman leads Red Buttons, the grandfather from *Willy Wonka and the Chocolate Factory*, a kid who isn't Charlie, and his older sister, Nancy Drew, to safety.

THE POSEIDON ADVENTURE

388.

Nancy Drew grows up, changes her name to Fallon, and moves to Denver where she, her sexually confused brother, and large extended family force shoulder pads down the throats of a once-innocent nation.

DYNASTY

389.

**Every mystery is perfectly solved
except George's orientation.**

THE NANCY DREW MYSTERIES

390.

Their playfully innocent post-mystery banter
and roughhousing make you feel both
very uncomfortable and
very happy.

THE HARDY BOYS

391.

The days seem happier than they actually were.

HAPPY DAYS

392.

Things will never be like they were.

393.

Things start to go very bad until
a passing ship saves the passengers.

LIFEBOAT

394.

No movie, TV show, book, or musical about the *Titanic* will end well.

395.

Will Smith and Charlize Theron are gods, and Jason Bateman gets totally screwed over.

HANCOCK

396.

The dog dies. Then Will Smith dies.

I AM LEGEND

397.

Will Smith's a robot.

I, ROBOT

398.

The farmer from *Babe* shuts down all the robots in the world, forcing people—including Bruce Willis's agoraphobic wife—to interact with one another for the first time in years.

SURROGATES

399.

Samuel Jackson caused all the disasters to lure Bruce Willis into being a hero.

UNBREAKABLE

400.

Bruce Willis is dead within the first few minutes.

THE SIXTH SENSE

ACKNOWLEDGMENTS

He's an agent who actually cares.

MITCHELL WATERS

He's an editor who is as sharp with a pencil as he is a quip.

JAMES JAYO

She offers invaluable guidance, incomparable hilarity,

and a dose of reality when needed most.

NELLIE KURTZMAN

He makes the world better.

DAVID ROSEN

I asked for fries with that.

ALL OF YOU WHO WERE MEAN TO ME IN HIGH SCHOOL

You spoil me.

YOU KNOW WHO YOU ARE.